All Scripture references taken from the KJV of the Holy Bible unless otherwise indicated.

Spirit of Death & the Grave Pass Over Me & My House: Let My People Go

Freshwater Press 2023

ISBN: 978-1-960150-64-6

Paperback Version

Copyright 2023

All rights reserved. No part of this book may be reproduced, distributed or transmitted by any means or in any means including photocopying, recording or other electronic or mechanical methods without prior written permission of the publisher except in the case of brief publications or critical reviews.

Contents

Old Pharaohs 5
Let My People Go 6
Then Came The Blood 14
Guilty or Not? 17
What You Get 20
Multiple Evil Covenants 24
Pursuers Unto Death 27
When I See the Blood 31
Prayers 35
Reverse Captivity 41
Break Covenants & Curses 45
Bind Triangular Powers 49
Salud! 56
Familiar Spirits 59
Evil Summons 66
Charms 86
Dismantle Weapons 87
Greek Mythology 97
Divorcing Death 99
Closing Prayers 107
Acknowledgements: 115
Other books by this author: 116

Spirits of Death & the Grave Pass Over Me & My House:
Let My People Go

Freshwater Press, USA

This is a prayer book with some information at the beginning, but mostly it is a prayer book. The prayers in the book occupy approximately 70 pages. It is no small matter to get *Death* and the *Grave* to pass over you and your house unless God is invoked and involved in it. Also **you** have to make declarations and decrees to the powers of darkness to **make** them leave you alone.

Once you get to the prayers, open your mouth and just pray!

LIVE!

Old Pharaohs

When Israel was in Egypt land...Let My People Go! Let My People Go! So then God sayeth: 'Go down, Moses Way down in Egypt land Tell old Pharaohs to Let My People Go!' So Moses went to Egypt land...Let My People Go!

He made all Pharaohs understand...Let My People Go! Yes The Lord said 'Go down, Moses, Way down in Egypt land Tell old Pharaohs to, Let My People Go! Thus spoke the Lord, bold Moses said: Let My People Go!
'If not I'll smite, your firstborns dead' Let My People Go!

God, the Lord said 'Go down, Moses, Way down in Egypt land Tell all Pharaohs to, Let My People Go!' Tell all Pharaohs
To Let My People Go.

Paul Robeson

Let My People Go

Afterward Moses and Aaron went to Pharaoh and said, "This is what the Lord, the God of Israel, says: 'Let my people go, so that they may hold a festival to me in the desert.'" Pharaoh said, "Who is the Lord, that I should obey him and let Israel go? I do not know the Lord and I will not let Israel go.

(Exodus 5:1-2 NIV)

Pharaoh cannot be begged; he cannot be pacified or reasoned with; he is stubborn and relentless. He cannot be appealed to; he only answers to ***death***. Until the Angel of Death visited Pharaoh, he did not agree to let the Hebrews go out of slavery. Because he would not budge in his resolve, Pharaoh perished in the Red Sea. Death is the answer to any Pharaoh-like situation. Well, almost any – the Pharoah over Joseph, relented after having thrown Joseph in jail, he later got him out of jail and promoted Joseph.

God sent nine plagues to uncompromising Pharoah, and still he didn't give in, so God sent a tenth plague. A plague is as widespread and lasts as long as God says it will last. Sometimes it is until people learn their lesson and change their ways. However, some people will never give in, so they die.

> For I will pass through the land of Egypt this night and will smite all the firstborn in the land of Egypt, both man and beast; and against all the gods of Egypt I will execute judgment: I am the LORD.
>
> And the blood shall be to you for a token upon the houses where ye are: and when I see the blood, I will pass over you, and the plague shall not be upon you to destroy you, when I smite the land of Egypt.

If you live in the land of pharaohs and you know that you know that you are living upright before the Lord, by virtue of where you live, where you have chosen to live, or where you have found yourself living, you may be in harm's way. You could be guilty by associating with certain people if God hates them. If embedded in the land, you could have made alliances with them--, even married them. In so doing you could have adopted their habits and traditions. If in agreement, you may be complicit--, and straight up guilty.

When in Rome people don't just say they will do as the Romans, they actually do as the Romans. When they are in Vegas, they behave as if they are invisible and can get away with things because they think that no one knows them there.

Stubborn, hard-hearted Pharaohs think themselves *gods*, above regular people, but they are not. They are not God.

God is longsuffering, but God also knows that the unsaved people are doing what unsaved people do--, *unsaved stuff*. Evil people do what evil people do--, evil stuff. But when God has had enough, or when He hears your cry, He will act. God will not attack Pharoah for no reason. The Lord is a Man of War, but He doesn't attack for the sake of war.

When the Israelites were in Egypt, God sent plagues against the Egyptians and their land, for the sake of His people. God said He will reprove kings for your sake in Psalm 105:14. Verse 15 reads, *Touch not mine anointed.* Pharoah was a king, although he thought himself a *god*, so Jehovah reproved him--, 10 times, actually.

The Egyptians worshipped over 80 *gods*. They worshipped frogs, trees, the ox, ram, wolf, cat, cobra, vultures, and even Pharaoh himself. They worshipped pretty much everything they could SEE.

This did not escape God's view or purview. He knew what they were doing, and He let them worship those idols. However, God says He will reprove kings for your sake. It's when those idol worshippers started messing with God's people, and His people finally learned their lesson and cried out to God that Jehovah stepped in.

The Hebrews had been in Egypt for 400+ years and the prophecy was up. God's Mercy was again toward His people. Slavery is rough, but the Egyptians had made it unbearable. *They were oppressed so hard they could not stand,* so God sent a man, Moses, for the sake of the people to say to Pharoah, *"Let My people go."*

Pharaoh didn't. Not only were the Hebrews the work staff of a business called Egypt, but they were also **free** labor; they *were* the economy of Egypt. When Moses said, "Let God's people go," Pharoah surely heard, *Kiss your money and prosperity goodbye.*

Before the appointed time had come, God was not, on a regular basis, sending plagues to Pharoah or the land that Pharoah ruled. Egypt was prospering, big time, on the backs of the Hebrew slaves. God knew what Pharoah was doing; God knows, sinners are going to sin.

But time was up. When Pharaoh would not obey God – relent, or compromise, God sent plagues over Egypt.

The 10 plagues of Egypt in order are:

Water turning to blood, frogs, lice, flies, livestock pestilence, boils, hail, fire and thunder, locusts, and the ninth was darkness. Nine plagues before Pharaoh even began a partial bargaining. But he was not planning to allow them to take their animals.

The 10th Plague was the killing of firstborn children. These plagues were sent by God after Pharaoh refused to let the Hebrews leave Egypt.

If you're in the enemy's camp, you're captive. Without Jesus what happens ***in that camp*** also happens *to* you. In addition, what the captor does to you is also happening *to you*. Double trouble. <u>Unless Jesus.</u> Except by the Mercy of God, except by the Blood of Jesus all the things that God put on the Egyptians because it encompassed the entire land, those things will also happen to you.

If you are in a land or territory because you are **authorized** to be, then you have authority to pray and expect certain outcomes when you pray. If you are there illegally, you have no authority in that land. If you are captive, what can you do? If you *belong* in a territory, if you *belong* in a land, then you not only have authority, but you also have **responsibility** to pray for that land, to *heal* that land, spiritually speaking.

If you were Egyptian or belonged in Egypt, you should have been praying about 9 plagues ago.

Eight plagues ago – all the way from the first plague to the ninth Pharaoh could play dumb, pretending that he didn't know who God was talking about *letting go*. Pharoah could pretend that he didn't know **who** God was, oh wait, he did that, didn't he? After all Moses was raised up in the palace as Pharaoh's son; who could Moses be speaking *for*? Hardhearted Pharaoh could pretend, play dumb, play deaf and ignore Moses, after all, plagues were happening to everyone. Surely in the palace, Pharoah was insulated. The common people probably felt more pain from the plagues than the king, so what would he care?

Then Came The Blood

But then came The Blood, the Blood of the Lamb. Before the foundation of the world the Lamb was slain. The Blood of Jesus takes away the sin of the world. But the Blood of Jesus also delivers. The Better Blood, The Blood of Covenant was to be ours starting after Jesus died on the Cross at Calvary in the Gospels of the New Testament.

Starting in the Old Testament, the Blood **spoke**. The Blood told who was of the household of faith, who were the believers, the true people of God. It wasn't the actual Blood of Jesus yet, but it was the representation of The Better Blood.

By the time the Hebrews gathered to get out of Egypt and to the Red Sea, yes, Pharoah's army was pursuing, but they were an army of disconsolate, grieving men – all their first born were dead! *Well, possibly* they were grieving, remember Egypt is a land of hard hearts. Hard hearts are not only stubborn, but they also lack compassion. God knows that hearts are often hard, until the hardship or loss hits their house.

Some of the soldiers were firstborn in their families, so the army was already hit, even though it would be further decimated by the type and shadow of The Blood: the Red Sea. In all their warfare armor they were further weighed down in the Red Sea. The Word of God was not finished –, the plague was against *all* the first born, not just tomorrow night, or one day last week. There was no time stamp on it.

Spiritual warfare against a first born is serious, especially a first-born male, particularly the first-born male who opens the womb. First-borns are doubly blessed; they get all their parents' attention, and as I say of my oldest brother, they think they are running things, and often they are. They rule and enforce. Spending so much time with parents builds intelligence, discipline, and leadership qualities. Firstborns are highly favored and according to the Bible should be dedicated to the Lord.

Parents actually pay attention to them. I'm **not** a first born, so I know what I'm talking about.

Back to the Pharaoh problem: If your old Pharaohs won't let you go then do as God did in the Bible, send **all** this pestilence against him. If that doesn't work, if he still won't give in, then drown them in the Red Sea of the Blood of Jesus.

Guilty or Not?

Did the Hebrews worship Egypt's idol *gods*? Did their parents? They were there 430 years. God visits to the 10th even 14th generation of those that hate(disobey) Him. When the Hebrews lived in Israel, God told them over and over to stop worshipping idol *gods*, they did, they didn't, they did, they didn't – finally they got captured by those idol *gods* and were led away into hardened labor: slavery.

They were in trouble with God for worshipping idol *gods* and got captured by the people who serve probably those very same idol *gods*, so chances are pretty good that they hadn't learned their lesson and were more than likely guilty of serving idol *gods* of the land they were captive in. If for no other reason than to get along they may have continued to worship the same idols as Pharoah. However, if they were serving idol *gods*, when was Jehovah EVER going to hear and answer their cry to get out of captivity?

Exactly.

This is the same way today how humans, human souls, fragments of human souls get captured and taken away by the enemy. Sin. Sinning. Worshipping idols is chief among the sins.

Now the Hebrews are *captives*, hanging out in Egypt a land of lots of idol *gods*…seems like what they wanted at the time, but they were *oppressed so hard they could not stand.* So God sent Moses to say, *"Let My people go."*

If you can't conquer old *idols and get away from* old Pharaohs it may be because you made <u>covenant</u> with them, and they have become too familiar with you. As well, if you are serving idol *gods*, if you've made deals with them. If you have made covenant with them and you owe them worship.

Have you considered that the Pharaohs that you *used* to serve may have written a clause in the evil covenant that you two created, that if you ever stop serving them, that th*ey will do you in*? Even if they never wrote it down, is it *understood*?

Anything that is benefitting someone's flesh, they will not easily let it go, unless by force, or extreme and godly discipline. For example, food. Do you fast? Willingly or does someone have to **make** you "fast"? Know that what is benefiting or entertaining your flesh is usually diminishing you spiritually.

Let my people go.

You may want or need deliverance, but if you are *attached* to those idols you serve, they aren't going to leave easily. If you don't renounce them, if you don't break the covenant, they won't leave at all. This is one reason for prayer and fasting. Many only come out by prayer and fasting.

What You Get

Pharaoh, died in the Red Sea along with his army. They died because they were pursuing the Hebrews **unto death**. God deals with people according to their *plans* against you, according to their own hearts. And He will rebuke kings for the sake of His people. Pharoah adds serious emphasis to being *all in*.

How will you know if there is a **death covenant** in the evil covenant? You'd better believe there is. The cost of anything from the devil is **everything**. And, the covenant is **evil**.

The water turning into blood was Plague One, but they didn't seem to care. The plague of flies didn't seem to faze them. Locusts--, nope, frogs--, nope; that's the stuff they like.

Witchcraft people *play* with that stuff; it probably means nothing to them. Perhaps they were inconvenienced, probably scoffing and mocking God with words such as, "Is that all you've got?" **Pharaoh's court was filled with witchcraft** – remember the snakes?

They probably mocked God by saying, *those little plagues*? Pharaoh thought God wasn't going to do much more, or anything else, because these were *His* people, He wouldn't smite them, not His people. It is a tactic of war to use humans as a shield, but God sent nine plagues, that covered the land. The first nine plagues affected the Hebrews, also. But the 10th hit the Egyptians, only. The 10th didn't hit the Hebrews, because of **The Blood.**

Like the unbelieving genius who goes outside during violent thunderstorms cajoling God saying, *Bring it on,* while laughing in a storm that is showing the power of God. The same genius who can't figure out weeks or months later why his life is jacked up. God is not mocked. God has not lost His glory, so there is no reason to treat Him as if He had.

That guy was worshipping the *"storm gods."* Perhaps that was when he made a covenant that he didn't realize that he'd have to honor or pay in some other way, later. There *may not be* an immediate result to blasphemy, but God is not mocked.

Hard hearts--, arrogant, prideful, scornful people, are after the order of Pharoah.

Afflictions from childhood, stubborn afflictions, recurring afflictions, addictions that you thought were gone, but are back--, that's evil Pharaoh pursuing you; he will pursue you to death.

Make sure it is Pharaoh that dies, not you.

Pharaoh epitomizes the hardness of heart; it's the *spirit of pharaoh*. Many hardened criminals are under the control of the *spirit of pharaoh*.

An increase in suffering at the gate of deliverance is evidence. You're almost there,– and then you get pulled back, that's an old Pharoah, or pharaohs of your past. You think you're going to get free? God says you will.

Pharaoh is determined that you won't. Whose report will you believe?

The *spirits of mockery* and *arrogance* are the spirits *of pharaoh.* He is smug, disdaining and disrespectful. These are enemies who believe they can do anything and without impunity, as if they are impervious to the very things they dole out on others.

The *pharaoh spirit* wants you back in bondage and slavery, even if it means he has to go track you down and bring you back himself. Pharaohs want your worship, they want your work; they want free labor, where they get all the proceeds and rewards. Enemies who insult our God, enchanters, sorcerers, witchdoctors and diviners against us all have that haughty *spirit*, and are power struck, to some degree.

Pharaohs are hard taskmasters, control freaks, and destiny limiters who want to decide how far you can go saying, *"You can't leave, stay here and die."*

Multiple Evil Covenants

There are people who have entered into multiple covenants unconsciously; every time you take up or worship a new idol, you form a new covenant. If it is an idol, the covenant is automatically evil. Now there are dueling covenants. So we get saved, do we renounce and break the old covenants to form the Better Covenant. We should.

Covenants are made in very unsuspecting ways in the world in which we live, celebrity adoration, incisions on the body, native doctor rituals, or other rituals, drink a concoction, throw your clothes in the river, New Age practices, childhood games, vows, fraternity, sorority or secret society oaths. All this causes multiple problems of evil covenants and multiple altars working against you.

Multiple evil covenants mean multiple curses.

When Moses went to Pharaoh and pleaded to let the Israelites go, he said, "Who is the lord that I should obey his voice to let Israel go? I do not know the lord, nor will I let Israel go." That's another way of saying, *"I don't believe your god can do anything. I'll not stop attacking and oppressing you. Just get out."*

Could Pharoah, legally keep the Hebrews because they may be worshipping the same idols as the Egyptians? Could he keep them because they may have formed alliances, intermarried and adopted the culture of Egypt, thereby making covenant with the people and the land of Egypt?

Possibly, but God said, "Let My people go." To me, that means God was breaking all covenants with Egypt, for His people.

Pharoah may have also thought since he served so many *gods* that by sheer number, he might have some idol *god* in his pocket that would save him or let him continue to have his way. After all, God hadn't done too much to Pharoah, or Egypt in the last 430 years. Egypt was prospering and having its way in the world, even though they were serving a mish mash of idol *gods*.

Additionally, Pharaohs were worshipped as *gods*, themselves in ancient Egypt.

Pursuers Unto Death

Pharaohs believe they own people, or they have the right to do as they choose no matter how it affects anyone else. They don't even listen to **God** when He says: *Let My people go.* Death is the language of pharaohs, and their evil, idol *gods,* their uncompromising cohorts and understudies understand, and they are probably still be arguing in hell, once they get there.

Biblical Egyptian model: they don't mind pitting people against each other if it will get the result they desire. Chaos is fine with them.

- The *gods* I used to serve before coming out of sin, coming out of the world, coming *to* Christ, that are pursuing me to impart unto me their nature, be drowned in the Red Sea and die, in the Name of Jesus.

These demons have escalated now, they aren't just pursuing you, they want to take you out – because of that **Serve-Them-Unto-Death-Clause** in the evil, hidden covenant that you made knowingly or unknowingly with the devil—I mean, Pharoah. The ones that want to take you out are the ones whose **slaves** you used to be.

Egyptians, oppressors and captors may say things like, *"Oh, you don't want to be our slaves anymore? Then we will* **make** *you continue to serve us!"*

This happens in the same way that gang members can't jump out of gangs, street walkers can't walk away from a pimp without hearing, *"You belong to me, or you owe me."* How will a person just walk away from the Mafia? You can't just walk away–, at least that's what we've seen in the movies. Cult groups and occult groups, you can't just walk away. You either know all their secrets now, or you owe them money, and or service (worship).

Abusive spouses- come on, there is too much domestic violence for that very reason: one of them wants to leave the other--, and live!!

Plantation slaves, other kinds of slaves... really? You think you can *walk off a plantation*? Those who **used to be** your master, especially slave masters usually don't get the memo that ***it's over***. Or, they pretend they didn't get it. They choose not to accept it.

Maybe you've noticed that people who work in an entry level job, who get educated, will leave that place and go to *another* company or workplace because people are used to you in that entry position. They like you there. That's the *spirit of pharaoh*; it is anti-promotion.

Slave masters like it when you're a slave and they are the master. It is what is wrong with a lot of the world--, even today.

God will tell people to leave a place and go elsewhere so they can live, in a New York minute – He did it regarding Abraham.

More than once, God told someone in the Bible to take a different road back from a place than they took to get to that place. We can use that in our life. When we reach a place of problems and issues, we must use a different road to get **_out_** of dilemmas than we took to get into it.

- Lord, take the mark of the slave off me. The mark, the tattoo, the branding, the slave garments, the smell, the *spirit of the slave*, take it off me in the Spirit, so that it quickly manifests in the natural, in the Name of Jesus. Amen.

When I See the Blood

God says, ***When I see The Blood, when I see The Blood, I will know you are one of Mine. When I see The Blood, even in the night, I will pass over***, says the Lord. The night is like day to the Lord and He can see The Blood. He said, ***When I see The Blood, I will pass over.***

Red is the color at the long wavelength end of the visible spectrum of light. It has a dominant wavelength of approximately 700 nanometers. The Blood of Jesus is long reaching and far-reaching. It can reach you wherever you are. The Blood of Jesus can reach anyone wherever they are in space and time. The Blood of Jesus has energy, power; it transcends space and time, it is still as powerful as it ever was, even since that first drop that was shed in His Passion for us and at Calvary.

Red symbolizes life, health, vigor, war, courage, anger, love and religious passion. The Blood of Jesus is all that, and more.

In the Gospels, it is the Blood of the Lamb that takes away the sin of the world. In the Old Testament, in the Book of Exodus is our type and shadow what the sacrificial lamb had to be--, a year old and male. It doesn't say firstborn, but a male lamb a year old is highly prized by the owners of that lamb. Sacrifice had to mean something to them. Jesus meant everything to God. How it must have grieved God's heart. Even though God loves us with undying and eternal love, no normal parent would want to sacrifice a child, even for another.

God didn't send an angel, a created being to ransom mankind from sin and death – He sent His Only Begotten Son, 100% man and 100% God, because of the Blood. God **had** to see the Blood. If God could hear Abel's blood, a son of man, made entirely of flesh, a son of Adam and Eve, when God's own Son's blood was shed, **God HAD to know it.**

The evil Pharaohs and unrepentant enemies may be out for blood – and we've got some blood for them, the Better Blood. Blood of Jesus, answer for us, in the Name of Jesus.

Jesus came that we may have life and have it more abundantly.

- Every old Pharaoh, that is still pursuing me, die, in the Name of Jesus.

Pharaohs pursue unto **death**, even if you are saved. Even though you've accepted Jesus as your Lord and Savior, they don't stop until you MAKE THEM STOP. This is why our prayers have to be violent. The Kingdom of God suffers violence, and the violent take it by force.

Even though you are in the Kingdom, and it's been some time now, maybe years, all that stuff you used to do is pursuing you, trying to tempt you, trying to pull you back into the *world*, into Egypt, and into sin.

Listen: if you won't go back, they (Pharaoh and other unrepentant enemies) consider you runaway, like a runaway slave; they will pursue you unto death. They want to capture you and bring you in--, dead or alive. An APB is out against you, in the spirit. It is against your freedom, and your life, if necessary. You must resist that devil, pray violent prayers, fast--, and **live**! Amen.

Today is your day to use the prayers in this book to declare and decree, mightily, against the *spirit of death and the grave* that Pharaoh does not mind invoking against you.

Prayers

This could take a while... those who want to **live** will not care how long this takes.

**"Holy Ghost Fire –, fall (X5).
My life, receive Fire, become Fire.**

Lord, relieve me of this bondage and every yoke of bondage, in the Name of Jesus. I repent of every sin--, my own sins and the sins of my ancestors.
Lord, I repent of evil and reject evil foundation, in the Name of Jesus.

In the full armor of God, the Helmet of Salvation, the Breastplate of Righteousness, my loins are gird about with Truth, my feet are shod with the preparation of the Gospel of Peace. Lord, I take up the Shield of Faith to quench every fiery dart of the wicked one and the Sword of the Spirit, which is the Word of God. Lord, I am covered in the Blood of Jesus. I am clad in the Cloak of Zeal and garments of vengeance.

Lord, I plead Mercy from You, the Maker of Heaven and Earth, and I cry out for judgement against every evil pursuer of my life, in the Name of Jesus.

Any wicked power standing to interfere in this prayer, I bind you, in the Name of Jesus.

Any wicked power standing to intercept my prayers, I bind you, in the Name of Jesus.

Any wicked power standing to block this prayer, I bind you, in the Name of Jesus.

Lord, my God, let Fire from Heaven rain upon every black collar witch, occult man, sorcerer, diviner, or magician employed against my life and family. Let Fire also rain on every person, evil or ignorant, who is engaging the services of witches and agents of darkness for gray collar witchcraft against me, in the Name of Jesus Christ.

Today, Lord, I speak directly to all *pharaoh spirits* and Pharoah-like *spirits* operating against my life, health, finances, education, career, profession, ministry, marriage, children, family, and freedom to worship God.

Father, I ask, I implore You, do not sanction their wickedness against me, my life and destiny. I bind them and cast them into the Abyss from where there is no return, in Jesus' Name.

Every stubborn, unrelenting pursuer of my life and destiny be swallowed by the Earth; may the Earth open up and swallow you to desolation and destruction.

First, drown in the Sea of Judgment, as the Red Sea, to every *spirit of a pharaoh* from my family or strangers, perish in the Red Sea of Judgment in Jesus' Name.

I apply the Blood of Jesus over the doorposts and the lintels of my house.

I apply the Blood of Jesus over the doorposts and lintels of my heart.

I apply the Blood of Jesus over the doorposts and lintels of my mind, soul, body, and spirit, in the Name of Jesus.

I apply the Blood of Jesus, thank You Jesus, over my entire life, in the Name of Jesus.

Father, thank You, for You are the God who gives me life. Father, because of Your Mercy I am alive and well today, in the Name of Jesus.

I reject the *spirit of untimely death* in my life, in any form. I reject incidents, accidents, disease, infirmity, mysterious or sudden death, in the Name of Jesus.

Every *spirit* of untimely death in my life, the Lord Jesus rebuke you, and I reject you now in the Name of Jesus. Be ejected from my life and cast into the Abyss where there is no water, and from which there is no return, in Jesus' Name.

I reject untimely death in my family, and I break every covenant in my bloodline that would even remotely allow it, in Jesus' Name.

I reject untimely death in my children, in the Name of Jesus and I break every evil covenant that would even remotely allow it.

I apply the Blood of Jesus upon my forehead and on the forehead of my loved ones; *spirit of death* you must pass over, in Jesus' Name.

The Blood of Jesus can never be washed off my body, soul, spirit, or life, in the Name of Jesus.

Every arrow of death sent in my direction, back to the sender, in the Name of Jesus.

I decree my deliverance from every form of disease and sickness, in Jesus' Name.

No sickness is permitted to take my life. I shall not be a victim of sickness unto death, in the Name of Jesus.

I decree and I declare that I shall celebrate a long and healthy life in this Earth, in health, vitality, and in prosperity, until I am satisfied, in the Name of Jesus.

I break every evil pattern of untimely death in my family, I break it right now, in Jesus' Name.

I break the family bondage; I renounce and repent for the sin that caused the evil covenant that keeps the bondage in place. Lord, by Your Mercy, forgive the bloodline iniquity.

By the Blood of Jesus, I break the curse that keeps the bondage in place.

Father, I break the yoke that enables the bondage. I bind the demons that are sent to enforce the evil covenant, in the Name of Jesus.

Jesus, set us free, because who You set free is free, indeed!

Reverse Captivity

I undo everything that the enemy has done to me, by the Blood of Jesus. Lord, redeem the time and restore the years. Amen.

I deprogram every curse and I dismantle it, in the Name of Jesus.

I break and revoke all evil covenants, spells, chants, affirmations, incantations behind any evil, magic, evil works, and manipulations by the enemy, in the Name of Jesus.

Every evil entity and to the enemies of God, every evil human agent, I declare:

I am not your slave. I am not your captive. I do not owe you anything. I do not owe you any worship, I do not owe you any money, I do not owe you my life, or any part of it, in the Name of Jesus.

You do not own my life, or any part of it, in the Name of Jesus. Hands off me and my life, forever, in the Name of Jesus.

Pull out the hidden documents, expose them to the light of Jesus Christ, expose them to the Blood of Jesus and blot out all evil, hidden, lying, binding, slavery and slave master covenants, blot out all forever and infinity clauses, I nullify the agreements my ancestors made with You, by the Blood of Jesus.

I blot out the handwriting of my ancestors and my own signature, if applied knowingly or unknowingly, with the Blood of Jesus.

Father: see the Blood of Jesus and negate, nullify, and end every evil covenant, in the Name of Jesus. Amen.

I close up every dimensional access point that every enemy has to me with the Blood of Jesus and seal each one by the Holy Ghost--, above, below, to the east, north, south, west, in every direction and dimension, realm, timeline and age, in the Name of Jesus.

I break, revoke, and return every spell, and every curse back to the sender--, immediately-now, in the Name of Jesus.

I break, revoke and remove all curses, all evil weapons, evil covenants, spells, chants and enchantments, incantations, hex, vex, hoodoo, voodoo, all sorcery of any kind, and negative affirmations against me, in the Name of Jesus. I send the demon behind the curse back to its sender, in the Name of Jesus.

Powers pursuing good things prematurely in my life; die, in the Name of Jesus.

I cancel all evil covenants, including covenants within covenants, fine print, especially death vows, to-the-death covenants, perpetually, forever, and so on.

I cancel, dismantle, and revoke all curses against me and my life, in the Name of Jesus.

I send the curse and the demon attached to it to enforce it back to sender, in the Name of Jesus.

I bind up every attack against me because of my being saved and in the Kingdom of God. I bind up every attack against my purpose, ministry, and destiny, in the Name of Jesus.

Blood of Jesus, cover me, Amen.

Break Covenants & Curses

Lord if or where there are multiple evil covenants and multiple curses, I break them all.

- Every hidden covenant in my life, break by the power in the Blood of Jesus.

Breaking Curses

I bind every demon and every unclean *spirit* behind any evil work that has been devised against me. I send them back to where they came from, to their sender, in the Name of Jesus.

I nullify all evil spiritual energy behind every spell against me, in the Name of Jesus.

I break the evil covenant keeping the spell in place, in the Name of Jesus. I plead the Blood of Jesus to work against the demon behind the spell, in the Name of Jesus. I revoke the spell, in the Name of Jesus.

I am clad in the whole armor of God and I use every divine spiritual weapon of God against this and every demon, in the Name of Jesus.

I command the demon and the curse to go back to the sender, in the Name of Jesus. Lord God, deposit Your heavenly salt in my foundation to heal it, in the Name of Jesus.

My vehicle of destiny, I *loose* you from every bondage today, in the Name of Jesus. I proclaim my vehicle of destiny will not burn, it will not catch on fire, and it will not burn up, in the Name of Jesus. I dismantle every bondage, in the Name of Jesus.

I bind the demonic *spirit* and the power behind it--, behind every bondage.

I nullify the spiritual energy behind the bondage, in the Name of Jesus.

I break the evil covenant that is keeping the bondage in place, in the Name of Jesus.

I plead the Blood of Jesus against the demonic *spirits* behind the bondage and render them powerless, in the Name of Jesus.

I revoke the spell behind the bondage. I use all suitable divine, spiritual weapons against these demons. I dismantle, deprogram, and scatter the bondage, in the Name of Jesus.

I come against every bondage of my finances. I come against the bondage of poverty.

I come against the bondage of sin and death. I come against graveyard and imprisonment bondages, and every bondage of my vehicle of destiny, evil cauldron bondages, and paralysis and barrenness bondages, in Jesus' Name.

I also come against oppression and opposition bondages, no helpers, and no-mercy bondages, in the Name of Jesus.

I break collective captivity bondages.

I break sickness and illness bondages.

I break weakness and tiredness bondages.

I break closed heavens bondages. I break closed-doors bondages, in Jesus' Name.

I remove all evil marks. I bind the demons behind them. I terminate the evil spiritual energy behind them, and I break the evil covenant keeping those covenants in place, in the Name of Jesus.

I come against all evil marks; I use the Blood of Jesus against them. I revoke and unravel all the spells behind every evil mark in Jesus' Name.

I dismantle, deprogram, and scatter every evil mark against me, in the Name of Jesus.

I command the demons to come out and depart, in the Name of Jesus.

I proclaim that the Blood of Jesus washes the evil marks off of my body, spirit, and soul, forever, in the Name of Jesus.

I bind the unclean *spirits* of rejection, disfavor, hatred, revulsion, and extreme dislike targeted against me caused by every evil smell, in the Name of Jesus.

Bind Triangular Powers

Lord, arise and contend with those who contend with me, in Jesus' Name.

Anything in me that is blocking You, Heavenly Father, from fighting for me, have it come out of me right now. Come up and out, in the Name of Jesus. (X3)

I take authority over the effects of the elements, especially the *Triangular Powers*--, the sun, the moon and the stars, in the Name of Jesus.

Any evil using *Triangular Powers* to attack me, die, in the Name of jesus.

Let the eveningtide, take hold of the ends of the Earth, and shake the wicked out of it, in the Name of Jesus.

Earth and all celestial bodies, receive heavenly instruction on my behalf, in the Name of Jesus.

I command my morning--, that it is holy, in the Name of Jesus; therefore my entire day will be holy.

I prophesy the will of God to the morning, the first light will shake wickedness out of the Earth.

I command the night, in the Name of Jesus and declare that no evil power, ruler or principality, hex, vex, incantation, voodoo, hoodoo, or other black arts, astral projection or other telepathic evil will befall me, in the night, in the Name of Jesus.

I declare neither the sun, the moon, or the stars will smite me today, in the Name of Jesus.

I declare that no evil desire against me will come to pass, and I forbid all warfare, evil and corruption of others from transferring to me, in the Name of Jesus.

Womb of the morning, gestate good things for me, in the Name of Jesus.

I rebuke every creeping *spirit* against me at night, in the Name of Jesus.

I will not be afraid of the evil arrows that fly at noon day, in the Name of Jesus.

I bind and rebuke, the pestilence that walks in darkness, in Jesus' Name. I rest in safety at night because the Lord gives me sleep.

Lord, have Your angels guard and protect me. Give me deliverance and healing in the night season.

I command every demon that threatens my life to go back to the dry place, to the Abyss from where there is no water and no return, in the Name of Jesus, go, go, into the Abyss from where you cannot return.

I disconnect all evil against me from their network of powers. I disconnect their power from the powers of fire, the powers of wind, the powers of the sky and the powers of the Earth, and beneath the Earth, in the Name of Jesus.

Lord, cut off their powers from all *Triangular Powers* working against me, in the Name of Jesus.

By Thunder, by Fire, I break up every evil altar erected against me, in the Name of Jesus.

Every evil person, entity, or power that is working against my life, my health, my success, marriage, family, Lord Jesus, cut off their power from the powers of all the elements and the *Triangular Powers,* in the Name of Jesus.

Every evil incantation triangulated with the *Triangular Powers*--, the sun, moon, stars, water, earth, fire, pot, or charm against me, be cancelled and nullified by the Blood of Jesus.

Every witchcraft kitchen cooking up evil food for me, catch fire and burn all the way down, in the Name of Jesus. Lord, I break their power from all powers of the Earth, soil, stones, mountains, trees, rocks, in the Name of Jesus.

I disconnect their power from the network of other witchcraft *spirits*, scatter them that they never reconnect again, in the Name of Jesus.

Lord, cancel every satanic decree against my life by the power, in the Blood of Jesus Christ. Amen.

In the Name of Jesus, Lord put a hedge of Fire around me--, a wall of Fire, a mountain of Fire.

Make me too hot for my enemies to even come close to me, in the Name of Jesus, by Fire.

My life, be charged with the Fire of God, make my life so hot that no demon can touch it, in the Name of Jesus.

Every sleight of hand of the devil, every trick of the devil against me, Lord God, expose it. Show me, then cancel all his tricks against me, in the Name of Jesus.

Evil charms demonically charged by *Triangular Powers*, I command you to lose all potency against me, in the Name of Jesus, and return to sender.

Every charm programmed against me. I deprogram you, in the Name of Jesus.

Lord, for every charm that is employed against me, I shut every door and block all access points to me in every dimension, timeline, age, and realm by the Blood of Jesus, in the Name of Jesus.

Fire of God, I call down Fire, Fire, Fire, Fire against every evil altar erected or working against me or my bloodline, in the Name of Jesus.

Fire, Fire, Fire, I call down Holy Ghost Fire.

Lord, I repent of ancestral worship. I bind every ancestral *spirit*, power, and strongman from operating against my life and destiny, in the Name of Jesus.

Pharaoh of my father's house, of my mother's house, of my in-law's houses, of my Ex's houses: Die, in the Name of Jesus.

Parents, siblings and relatives who don't understand or approve that I won't follow the idols of my father's or my mother's house, I pray for your salvation, deliverance and understanding to be opened, in the Name of Jesus.

Ladders of Pharaoh in my life, be dismantled and scatter, in the Name of Jesus.

Stubborn tormentors assigned against my destiny! Die, in the Name of Jesus: I and my family will not be used as sacrifice, by the power in the Blood of Jesus.

Lord, release confusion and infighting among my enemies to their total destruction, in the Name of Jesus.

Lord, I require seven-fold restoration of all that has been stolen from me by my enemies--, especially those using ***Triangular Powers***, in the Name of Jesus.

Salud!

I shake all plans of infirmity planned against me, in the Name of Jesus.

I vomit up all polluted food from the sleep and the dream declaring it will have no effect on me, in the Name of Jesus.

Lord, heal me of every effect of evil night feedings, in the dream, in the spirit, in the Name of Jesus.

Lord, shake all long-time affliction out of my system, in Jesus' Name.

Multiple networks of automatic arrows targeted at me, backfire, in Jesus' Name. (X7)

Every demonic utterance spoken to me, at me, or against me, choke on your words; backfire, in the Name of Jesus.

Witchcraft sicknesses stealing my finances, wasting my time, and causing pain and discomfort, die by Fire, in the Name of Jesus.

Any witchcraft affliction put on me at birth, be nullified now, in the Name of Jesus.

Any sickness programmed to send me to the grave, I deprogram you, I dismantle your enchantment, I destroy your calendar and your clock, by the Blood of Jesus, in the Name of Jesus.

Evil agenda to put me on a sick bed or a bed of affliction, expire, and you take that sick bed. Backfire, in the Name of Jesus.

Bacteria, virus, fungus, parasites, afflictions, disorders, diseases, symptoms, syndromes, incidents, accidents, mishaps, and mistakes sent against me, expire now; return to sender, in Jesus' Name.

Power of God, uproot generational sickness from my life, in the Name of Jesus.

Every arrow of sickness and death, return to sender, in the Name of Jesus.

I break every cycle of sickness and affliction against me, my life, or my family, in the Name of Jesus.

Familiar Spirits

Familiar spirit arrows targeted at me to end my life, backfire, in the Name of Jesus.

Vultures of death, backfire by the power in the Blood of Jesus, in the Name of Jesus.

Arrows of automatic failure targeted against my life, backfire, in the Name of Jesus. (X5)

I resist and reject every killer disease, in the Name of Jesus.

Lord, I receive the resurrection power of the Lord Jesus Christ, in Jesus' Name.

I inhale the Fire of God and exhale out every infirmity, in the Name of Jesus.

Evil imagination of death for my life, backfire to sender, in the Name of Jesus.

Power assigned to trouble me in my dreams, die, in the Name of Jesus.

I speak life to myself and destruction to all my enemies and all their weapons, in Jesus' Name.

I paralyze the activities of household wickedness, in the Name of Jesus.

Every vulture of death circling around my life, receive Holy Ghost Fire, crash and burn, in the Name of Jesus.

Witchcraft powers that have captured my health, release me now, in the Name of Jesus.

Blood of Jesus, purge my body and blood from every witchcraft-sponsored infirmity, in the Name of Jesus.

I enter into Divine Health Covenant with God for my life, in the Name of Jesus. Lord, let it work for me, in the Name of Jesus. My life is covered by the Blood of Jesus.

I declare, I will not die prematurely; I will not die before my time. I refuse to be killed or limited by any sickness, infirmity, or disease in any form. I refuse to die by enemy attack, in the Name of Jesus.

I break every plot of the enemy against me, in the Name of Jesus.

Hell, grave, covens, human evil agents--, every evil agenda against me is arrested now, in the Name of Jesus.

I abort every evil conception against me, in the Name of Jesus.

I overturn every chariot of every evil Pharaoh into the Red Sea, in the Name of Jesus.

Like Pharaoh's army's chariots, I overturn every wicked plan of the enemy against me, in the Name of Jesus.

Every unrelenting Pharaoh pursuing me, I bind you and send every plague, disease, pestilence, inconvenience and setback--, BACK to the sender, as the Lord sent Egypt, in the Book of Exodus. Be perpetually drowned in the Red Sea.

Every demonic plot is miscarried and aborted, and I silence the mocking voices against me, in Jesus' Name.

I release myself and family from all witchcraft blood covenants, in the Name of Jesus.

Thunder of God, roll and destroy every stronghold of darkness mounted against me, in the Name of Jesus.

Every arrow of untimely death, jump out and return to senders, in the Name of Jesus.

Blood of Jesus, wash away every strange touch, every evil touch against my life, in the Name of Jesus.

Lord, by Your power, purge my blood of every evil injection.

Stones of Fire, strike every evil vulture, and let them fall down and die, in the Name of Jesus.

I silence all evil altars speaking against my life, in the Name of Jesus. Blood of Jesus, answer for me.

Any part of my body that has been spiritually sacrificed to the devil, I take you back, I repossess you, in the Name of Jesus, by the power of the Only Living God.

All arrows from the occult against my health-- back to senders, in Jesus' Name.

I bind and cast out any deposit of darkness, in the Name of Jesus.

My life, my body, become too hot for witchcraft powers, in the Name of Jesus.

Any demon assigned to kill me, fall down and die, in the Name of Jesus.

My soul, my spirit, do not answer any evil call, summons or instruction, in the Name of Jesus.

Enemies of God:

I am not your slave. I am not your captive. I do not owe you anything. I do not owe you any worship, I do not owe you any money, I do not owe you any service. I do not owe you my life, or any part of it, or the lives of my children, family or generations--, forever, in the Name of Jesus.

You do not own my life, or any part of it, in the Name of Jesus. I belong to Christ; I am His bondservant, friend and child of the Most High God.

You owe me 7-fold of everything you've ever stolen from me, in the Name of Jesus.

Father, anoint my feet to go to the right place at the right time, forever, in the Name of Jesus.

Every evil sacrifice speaking against my life, be nullified, in the Name of Jesus.

I reject any deadly attack prepared for me or my family, in the Name of Jesus.

Lord, **_see_** The Blood and let *death*, dread, disease and sickness pass over me and my family, my house, in the Name of Jesus. (X3)

My head, reject bewitchment, in the Name of Jesus.

I break every evil covenant that allows my blood to have witchcraft markers in it. My blood, reject bewitchment, in Jesus' Name.

Every organ in my body, reject bewitchment, in the Name of Jesus.

My head, hands, legs, are not available for evil sacrifice, in the Name of Jesus. I am a child of the Most High God, and I am an heir of Abraham. I am a victor, not a victim, in the Name of Jesus.

Evil Summons

My spirit, refuse to go to any graveyards, grave sites, cemeteries, coven meetings, evil satanic circles via evil summons, in the Name of Jesus.

Heavenly Father, deliver me from the grip of household wickedness, in the Name of Jesus.

Every evil force assigned to destroy me from ancestral altars, fall down and die, in the Name of Jesus.

Every angel of darkness assisting my household enemies, fall down and die, in the Name of Jesus.

Every evil covenant that is promoting curses in my life, break, in the Name of Jesus.

Every evil gang-up in my place of birth that is set up against my life, scatter in shame, in the Name of Jesus.

Every wicked strongman of my father's or mother's house, fall down, and die, in the Name of Jesus.

Every *spirit of Cain* assigned to waste my destiny, be wasted yourself, in the Name of Jesus. Any power outside my family that is sponsoring attacks against my life, be exposed to death, in the Name of Jesus.

Every evil arrow that is fired into my life from my place of birth, backfire, in the Name of Jesus.

O Lord, arise in Your anger and deliver me from household wickedness, in the Name of Jesus.

Every curse placed upon my life from my blood relations, die immediately, in the Name of Jesus. I cut myself off from any communal bondage, in the Name of Jesus.

Any evil power in my family, prospering with my destiny, die, in the Name of Jesus.

Any *stranger*, any whosoever prospering with my destiny, die, in the Name of Jesus.

Heavenly Father, deliver me completely from enemies that I would never suspect or see as enemies – the ones that are very close to me, in the Name of Jesus.

Any evil personality in my family that has vowed to destroy me, fail woefully, and in shame, in the Name of Jesus.

Every enchantment, curse and spell that is working against me, backfire, in the Name of Jesus.

Let the Goliath of my father's house fall down and die now, in the Name of Jesus.

Every evil tongue that is speaking against my life, be silenced forever, in the Name of Jesus.

Let every devourer in my family be devoured by Fire, by force, in the Name of Jesus.

I shall not bow down to the powers of darkness in my household, in the Name of Jesus.

I break and *loose* myself from all attacks of household powers, in the Name of Jesus.

Every evil utterance said against me by the evil powers of my father's house, mother's house, in-laws' houses, relatives houses, Ex's houses or their compatriots, die, in the Name of Jesus.

Let hidden curses in my life that are causing me to suffer, be exposed, dismantled, and reversed, in the Name of Jesus.

Every hidden curse in my life, your time is up, die, in the Name of Jesus.

Every inherited curse of poverty in my life, die, in the Name of Jesus.

Blood of Jesus, speak destruction unto every spell in my life, by the power of the Name of Jesus.

I cancel every evil handwriting that is against me, in the Name of Jesus.

Every stubborn curse that is placed upon my life since I was a baby, die, in the Name of Jesus.

Every hidden curse that I inherited from my parents, receive Holy Ghost pink slip – you are FIRED, by Holy Ghost Fire, in Jesus' Name.

Every inherited evil covenant in my life be broken, in the Name of Jesus.

Every evil ancient covenant that keeps an inherited curse of untimely death in my family's bloodline, or in my life, die, in the Name of Jesus.

Any strongman, following me about because of ancestral curses, fall down and die, in the Name of Jesus.

Any inherited curse from my parents assigned to harm me or destroy me, my life is not available--, die, in the Name of Jesus.

Any hidden curse that has been placed upon me, because of an agreement of any kind, in a dream, die, in the Name of Jesus.

O Lord, reveal to me all my hidden problems and destroy them, in the Name of Jesus.

Any strange sickness or problem in my life as a result of hidden curses, die with your curse, in the Name of Jesus.

You, the yoke of hidden curses in my life, break and lose your hold, in the Name of Jesus.

Every agent of hidden curses in my life, be exposed and die, in the Name of Jesus.

Every witchcraft curse that is attacking me from the dark, be exposed, and die, in the Name of Jesus.

Heavenly Father, deliver me from all types of hidden curses, in the Name of Jesus.

I break and loose my destiny from the destruction caused by hidden curses, in the Name of Jesus.

Every enemy of my destiny, wherever you are now, be intimidated, in the Name of Jesus.

By the power and the Word of God, I challenge every Goliath in my life, in the Name of Jesus. Father Lord, confront and conquer every enemy of my destiny, in the Name of Jesus.

Every satanic barrier that is blocking good things from my life, clear away by Fire, in the Name of Jesus.

Any power attacking me with fear, *you* receive fear and die by Fire, in the Name of Jesus. Jesus, speak fear into the camp of my enemies, in the Name of Jesus.

Any power assigned to manipulate my decisions fall and die by Fire, in the Name of Jesus.

Lord, let all demons that are working against my destiny be scattered by Thunder, in the Name of Jesus.

Blood of Jesus flow into the camp of my enemies and intimidate them, in Jesus' Name.

I reject every evil gift that has been assigned to intimidate me and divert my destiny, in the Name of Jesus.

Every inherited fear that is assigned to intimidate me, die by force, in Jesus' Name.

Any human altar burning incense against my life receive stroke, in the Name of Jesus.

Any evil diversion working against my life from the camp of the devil, die, in the Name of Jesus.

Let the evil altars of my father's house catch Fire by the Holy Ghost, in the Name of Jesus.

I command the Fire of God to burn every intimidating fear of the devil, in the Name of Jesus.

Blood of Jesus flow into my family altars and scatter every demon, in the Name of Jesus.

Any evil giant planted on my path to breakthrough, collapse and die, in the Name of Jesus.

Every intimidating voice of the wicked directed towards me, backfire, in Jesus' Name.

Every satanic angel assigned to intimidate me fall down and die, in the Name of Jesus.

Let my appearance before all my enemies intimidate them, by Fire, in the Name of Jesus.

Every giant, every strongman in my father's house that is standing against me, fall down and die, in the Name of Jesus.

Every fear that was programmed into my life move away, in the Name of Jesus.

Every evil tongue speaking against me, be silenced by the crying Blood of Jesus, in the Name of jesus.

Glory of God, arise and overshadow my life, let me dwell in the Shadow of the Almighty, in the Name of Jesus.

I command every witchcraft power working against my life to be destroyed, in the Name of Jesus.

Every altar of witchcraft in my father's house, scatter, in the Name of Jesus.

Let the strongman of my father's house using witchcraft against me, die, in the Name of Jesus.

Father Lord, by Your power, I command all those practicing witchcraft against me to become perpetually confused, in the Name of Jesus.

Holy Ghost Fire, burn every garden and grove of witchcraft, burn to ashes, in Jesus' Name.

Every instrument of witchcraft against my life catch fire, in the Name of Jesus.

Anointing to terminate witchcraft powers fall upon me now, in the Name of Jesus.

Blood of Jesus, pursue witchcraft powers in my life, to their death, in the Name of Jesus.

Heavenly Father, deliver me from every witchcraft power, in the Name of Jesus,

Every yoke of witchcraft in my life, break to pieces. Any evil personality that is into witchcraft because of me, fail, in the Name of Jesus.

Any witch or wizard ministering against God's purpose for my life, fail, in the Name of Jesus.

Let the chains of witchcraft that are holding me break now, in the Name of Jesus.

I command every stronghold of witchcraft to break by Fire, in the Name of Jesus.

Every arrow of witchcraft fired into my life, like a hot javelin, I throw you back, in the Name of Jesus.

Every judgment of witchcraft against my life, be reversed, in the Name of Jesus.

I reject every witchcraft load that is on my life, in the Name of Jesus.

Oh Lord, deliver me from witchcraft curses, in the Name of Jesus.

Every *marine spirit* altar of witchcraft, catch fire, in the Name of Jesus.

Blood of Jesus, flow into every throne of witchcraft.

Any witchcraft sickness in my life, die, in the Name of Jesus.

Every evil group gathering against my life, scatter by thunder, in the Name of Jesus.

Any evil crowd gathering against me, scatter, in the Name of Jesus.

Any chain of witchcraft chaining me together with evil people, break, in the Name of Jesus.

Any chain binding or chaining me to people under the Judgment of God, break, in Jesus' Name, and let me go. Let me go!

At the hand of the Holy Ghost, scatter the enemies of my soul, in the Name of Jesus

By the power of God. I scatter every evil gang up against my destiny, in the Name of Jesus.

Every stronghold of witchcraft against my life, collapse, in the Name of Jesus.

Every evil *marine* kingdom agent that is talking against my destiny, let its kingdom fail, in the Name of Jesus.

Any evil plan against my destiny fail totally, by Fire, in the Name of Jesus.

Let the mouths of wicked agents in any evil gathering be closed, in the Name of Jesus.

Gathering of demons against my life, catch fire, in the Name of Jesus.

Blood of Jesus flow into any evil group and destroy its plans against me, in Jesus' Name.

Let the ministry of evil gang up against my life, be terminated, in the Name of Jesus.

Unrelenting human persecutors, forget my name and lose my location, in Jesus' Name.

Lord, let all my enemies be confused in their meeting places, in the Name of Jesus.

Any curse of the enemy in my life, be roasted by Fire, in the Name of Jesus.

By the anointing of the Holy Ghost, I destroy every satanic gathering, in the Name of Jesus.

Every announcement in any evil meeting be cancelled, Lord, confuse their communication, in the Name of Jesus.

I reject and negate every evil agreement made against me, in the Name of Jesus.

Ancestral powers that have gathered together against me, Angels of War, put them to shame, in the Name of Jesus.

Lord Jesus, arise and disgrace my enemies, in the Name of Jesus.

Blood of Jesus, deliver me right now from every evil gathering, in the Name of Jesus.

Territorial witches working in this entire area – Lord, I plead The Blood, cover me in the Blood Of Jesus.

Lord, keep me out of wrong places at wrong times, today and forever, in the Name of Jesus.

Father, see The Blood, see The Blood of Jesus and let all evil, death, and punishment pass over me, even in the land of idols, even in the land of Pharaohs, even in the land of evil, arrogance, and indolence, in the Name of Jesus.

Lord, bind those witches, Lord, bind every evil human agent and forbid them from casting evil into the land today, tonight. Scatter their meeting, that they never reconvene, in the Name of Jesus.

Lord, see The Blood. See The Blood.

Blood of Jesus, cause the death angel to pass over me, my family, this house, in the Name of Jesus.

Blood of Jesus—speak, Blood of Jesus speak against every evil Pharaoh pursuing me for captivity, for evil, or unto death, in the Name of Jesus.

Blood of Jesus, speak me out of every blood sacrifice, holding me in bondage, in the Name of Jesus.

Any evil voice speaking against me from any evil altar or pit of hell, be silenced by the crying Blood of Jesus, in the mighty Name of Jesus.

Every legal right occultic agents have against me, be destroyed by the crying Blood of Jesus.

Any sin in my life energizing evil sacrifices to speak against me, be weakened unto death by the crying Blood of Jesus.

Every record of sin in my life, anywhere in creation, be removed, be expunged permanently by the crying Blood of Jesus.

Any animal or human sacrifice crying against my life, be silenced, by the crying Blood of Jesus Christ.

Wherever they will call my name or the name of my family members for evil, Blood of Jesus answer for us, in the Name of Jesus.

Heavenly Father, terminate every evil verdict and judgment pronounced against me by satanic agents from any evil altar or from any evil, satanic council, in the Name of Jesus.

Any man, woman, or power that has vowed to convert my life to nothing, be frustrated by the crying Blood of Jesus.

Every iniquity inviting demons into my life from any evil altar, Lord forgive me, and let that iniquity be destroyed by the crying Blood of Jesus, in the mighty Name of Jesus.

Any evil sacrifice offered to take me away from divine protection, expire, by the crying Blood of Jesus.

Angels of protection never leave me; Lord, give me a divine angelic detail. Lord let there be **no** unguarded moment in my life for the enemy to attack, in the Name of Jesus.

Any evil mark, or satanic identification mark in my life from satanic kingdom be erased by the crying Blood of Jesus, in Jesus' Name.

Any *strange fire* burning in my life from household witchcraft, quench by the crying Blood of Jesus.

Let the fear of me intimidate my enemies, by the power in the crying Blood of Jesus.

Blood of Jesus when my enemies hear of me, cause them to fear and tremble to defeat, in the Name of Jesus.

Any evil summons targeting my existence, fail woefully and backfire by the power, in the crying Blood of Jesus.

Every known and unknown curse against my destiny, come to an end, by the crying Blood of Jesus.

Any invitation given to the devil, demons and satanic agents from any evil altar, I withdraw you by the power in the Blood of Jesus, in the mighty Name of Jesus.

Every evil trap, accident, or death organized against me by any evil personality from satanic altars, catch your owners, by the power in the Blood of Jesus.

Ancient of Days, silence any and all blood sacrifices speaking against me from pagan and heathen altars, in the mighty Name of Jesus.

Any arrow of death and hell fired against me from any evil altar, backfire by the Blood of Jesus, in the Name of Jesus.

Heavenly Father, invoke The Blood of your firstborn Son, Jesus, to cry me out of every danger, in the Name of Jesus.

I break away and *loose* myself from every evil voice speaking against me from the grave.

Let the blood of animal sacrifices crying against me from the ground be silenced by the Blood of Jesus.

Any area of my life under satanic attack because of blood sacrifices, receive deliverance, in the Name of Jesus.

The Blood of Jesus, the Blood of the Firstborn has conquered both *Death* and the *Grave*, in the Name of Jesus.

Any evil sacrifice ever offered against my life by anyone, dead or alive, expire, in the Name of Jesus.

Any human sacrifice that is crying from my foundation, your time is up; close your mouth, in the Name of Jesus.

Every programmed infirmity in my life from *any* blood crying against me, be destroyed by the Blood of Jesus.

Wherever they will call my name for evil, Blood of Jesus, answer for me.

Spirit of Cain from any evil altar and with determination to kill me, fail, by the Blood of Jesus.

Every death *spirit* sent to kill me, go back to your sender, in the Name of Jesus.

Every weapon of death prepared against me because of my belief, my life, my purpose, my prayers, my destiny, turn against your owner, in the Name of Jesus.

Every sickness in my life, from any witchcraft, coven or altar, dry up with all your roots, in the mighty Name of Jesus.

I command every enchantment and divination against me from evil altars to expire by force, by Fire, in the mighty Name of Jesus.

Blood of Jesus shield my life against any evil sacrifice ever offered against my life.

Wherever they call my name for evil, Blood of Jesus, answer for me, in the mighty Name of Jesus.

Almighty God, deliver me from blood sacrifice that is crying against me, in the mighty Name of Jesus.

Any evil deposit in any organ of my body from any sacrificial crying blood, be superseded by the Better Blood, the Blood of Jesus.

Father: see The Blood!

Blood of Jesus, mediate between me and God and deliver me from the powers of sin, sickness, and disease.

Charms

Father: see The Blood and let all evil pass over me, my house, family, business, and life, in the Name of Jesus.

I belong to Christ and I'm *all in*, in the Name of Jesus.

Lord, raise up an adversary against my enemies, and destroy them, in the Name of Jesus.

I bind the *spirit of retaliation* and backlash and proclaim that no *spirit*, power, entity, or evil human agent will be able to retaliate against this prayer, in the Name of Jesus. Thank You, Lord, I count it as done, in the mighty Name of Jesus.

Dismantle Weapons

(Adapted from the book, <u>Consuming Fire for Fire</u> *by Reverend Kay El Blessing.)*

I disarm my enemies of all their weapons being used against me, in the Name of Jesus.

Holy Ghost Fire, burn them and their weapons, in the Name of Jesus.

Burn into ashes every weapon released against me in Judgment, in the Name of Jesus. I command the All-Consuming Fire to burn into ashes, every weapon of witchcraft, black magic, red magic, green magic, sorcery, voodoo, hoodoo, Santeria, Obeah curses and hexes being used against me and my family, in the Name of Jesus.

Let the Judgment Fire of God, disarm my enemies of all their weapons today, in the Name of Jesus.

From today I declare by the Fire of God that no enemy weapon formed against me, or my family shall prosper, in the Name of Jesus.

I command the spiritual and physical atmosphere to be on fire right now. I charge my surroundings with the Fire of God, in Jesus' Name.

I command evil networks to be paralyzed by Fire, now, in Jesus' Name.

Every monitoring device used against me be set on Fire, in Jesus' Name.

I command demons and unclean *spirits* working against my life and destiny from evil altars to be scattered by Fire, Holy Ghost Fire, in Jesus Name.

I command every strange gathering that is against me or my family to be scattered by Fire, in the Name of Jesus.

I set on Fire, the evil networks and projections against my life and destiny, in the Name of Jesus.

Every arrow that has been shot against my life, be canceled against me now, and return to sender, in Jesus' Name.

I release *Fire*. I release *Fire* on every enemy of my life, in the Name of Jesus.

I cancel all evil arrows against my household, and I set them ablaze, now, in the Name of Jesus.

I destroy, by Fire every witchcraft, hex, and spell released against me and my family, in the Name of Jesus.

Lord, drive out, by Fire, every sickness released against me, in the Name of Jesus.

Backfire, let every evil plan of the enemy against me backfire, in the Name of Jesus.

By Fire, I destroy the arrow of sorrow and disaster released against me. I destroy by Fire every arrow of disappointment released against me, in the Name of Jesus.

Holy Ghost, Fire: Burn it and let it burn. Burn, in the Name of Jesus.

In the Name of Jesus Christ, I renounce, break, and *loose* myself from all demonic subjection to all enchanters and enchantments, charms and charmers, or any other evil beings, living or dead that have dominated me. Thank You, Lord. Thank You, Lord. Thank You, Lord, for setting me free.

Ancient of Days turn me to Fire, in the Name of Jesus.

My life, receive Fire, become Fire, in the Name of Jesus. My life, receive Fire, become Fire, in the Name of Jesus. My life, receive Fire, become Fire, in the Name of Jesus. My life, receive Fire, become Fire, in the Name of Jesus.

I cancel every charm, spell, enchantment, and divination assigned against me, in the Name of Jesus.

Every evil cauldron working against me, receive the judgment of God, in the Name of Jesus.

Every evil word programmed into the sun, the moon, and the stars against me, backfire to sender, in the Name of Jesus.

Every evil load dumped on my back, I send you back to your owner --, carry your own load and get out of my life, in the Name of Jesus, Go! Go, in the Name of Jesus.

I repeal every evil agreement made in the dream, in the Name of Jesus.

Angels of Healing, derail attacks against my health, in the Name of Jesus.

Angels of War, pummel every enemy of my spirit, soul and body, by the smoke from the nostrils of God; here comes some smoke.

Lord, establish and send instruments of death, send plague and disaster against my unrelenting, unyielding pharaoh-like adversaries, in the Name of Jesus.

Angels of Protection lift me up so that I don't even dash my foot against a stone, in the Name of Jesus.

All weaponized demonic activity sent against me is sent back to the pit of hell, in the Name of Jesus.

Any fallen angels or malevolent *spirits* be apprehended by God's heavenly hosts before they ever arrive at my abode, in Jesus' Name.

I break **all** attempts at astral projection and evil psychic and telepathic activities and instructions sent toward me or against me, in the Name of Jesus.

Womb of the Morning, gestate wellness, wholeness, health, wealth and prosperity for me, in the Name of Jesus.

Every evil bird, every evil sign, symbol, and omen of death, dying, and the grave, I bind and paralyze you. I bind the screech owl and every hooting, talking, evil, or programmed owl or other fowl, in the Name of Jesus.

I bind the *spirit of death*, *dying* and the *grave*.

Every rooftop, treetop vulture, crow--, every unclean animal and foul *spirit*, you are bound from me and my house today, tonight, 24/7, in the Name of Jesus.

Every *pharaoh spirit* in my life, die, in the Name of Jesus.

Any witchcraft power that has refused to let me go, die immediately, in the Name of Jesus.

Let the judgment of God fall upon every evil power assigned to waste my life, in Jesus' Name.

Blood of Jesus, locate every stubborn problem in my life and destroy it, in the Name of Jesus.

You, Serpent--, I destroy your head that has been assigned to bite me to death, in Jesus' Name.

Every curse that is or has been placed on my life by the devil and his agents, catch fire, in the Name of Jesus.

I break and *loose* myself from every evil arrest of the enemy, in the Name of Jesus.

Any power that has vowed to kill me, the Lord Jesus rebuke you; die now, in the Name of Jesus.

Heavenly Father let Your strong Hand take me away from enemies and opponents, in the Name of Jesus.

Blood of Jesus, flow into my brain and deliver me by *Fire*, in the Name of Jesus.

Holy Ghost Fire, burn every enemy of my progress to ashes, in the Name of Jesus.

Any evil power that has risen up against me, be broken from your network and your power source, in the Name of Jesus.

Any witchcraft altar, against me, scatter, in the Name of Jesus. Let the strongman of my father's house die by Fire, in the Name of Jesus.

Angels of the Living God, arise and kill all representatives of Haman and every Pharaoh in my life, in the Name of Jesus.

I refuse to die. My uncompromising enemies shall die, not me, in the Name of Jesus.

Every yoke of untimely death that is placed on my life, I repent for the sin that created the evil covenant and brought the curse, whether myself or my ancestors. I break the curse, in the Name of Jesus. I bind the demon(s) sent to enforce the curse, in Jesus' Name. I break the bondage and the resultant yoke because of the evil covenant in the Name of Jesus.

Any power on suicide mission against my life, die alone, die before you ever reach me, in the Name of Jesus.

Let all representatives of Haman in my life die on their own gallows, and every Pharaoh drown in the Red Sea, in the Name of Jesus.

I command the *spirit of death* to die, to expire by the power in the Blood of Jesus that He shed for us in His Passion and on the Cross at Calvary.

All powers against my waking up: expire, in the Name of Jesus.

Every evil council meeting or coven gathering against me, I resist you; I send fog and confusion into your meetings. I plead the Blood of Jesus to answer for me, whenever you call my name or the name of my spouse, children or family. Scatter, in the Name of Jesus.

Let every messenger of death to announce my obituary in the spirit find me not, in the Name of Jesus. Announce your own death, not mine. I shall live and not die, in the Name of Jesus.

Blood of Jesus.

Blood of Jesus.

Blood of Jesus.

Lord, see The Blood and let *death* and the *grave* pass over me, my family, this house, my life, in the Name of Jesus.

Greek Mythology

This a brief mythology lesson to help understand the prayer that follows by Dr. Daniel Duvall: *Divorcing Death.*

Thanatos in Greek mythology is the personification of Death. **Hypnos** is his twin brother; hypnosis is ungodly sleep. You should never be hypnotized; it causes you to vacate your body. While you're not in your own body, the devil can put anything in there. Sorceries accomplish the same thing --, drugs and alcohol.

Nyx is night and he is allegedly the father of Thanatos.

Scotus (*Erebus, Erebos*) is darkness. ***Moros*** is doom. ***Kouros*** personifies destruction.

Morpheus was part of the ***Oneiroi***, who were dream spirits. *Morpheus* had the skill to influence the dreams of *gods* and kings. His brothers would visit the rest of mankind with ungodly dreams. I don't know of anyone who can boast of never having had an ungodly dream.

Momus is blame. ***Moirai*** is the fates.

Nemesis means indignation. ***Appetae*** is the --- Greek goddess of deceit. And ***Eris*** is the Greek goddess of strife and discord.

I add to this grouping any other evil entity, demon, spirit, principality, ruler or wickedness yet unknown or unpronounceable by me, in the Name of Jesus.

Divorcing Death

(This entire Divorcing Death prayer is from Dr. Daniel Duvall, Bride Ministries. **Amen? Means do you agree. Say** *I agree* **if you do.)**

Father God, I come before You in the mighty name of Jesus, Lord God, I thank You for Your presence, for Your angelic armies, that there are more with us than are with them.

I thank You, Lord Jesus that You have disarmed principalities and powers, triumphing over them, making an open show of them; you finished the work. And You will punish the hosts of the high ones that are on high, and the kings of the Earth.

You said that if two agree as touching, anything on Earth, You will do it for us in Heaven. And we thank You for safety in the atmosphere, in the name of Jesus.

Finally, God, we list the following entities and refer to them as The Group: *Thanatos, Nyx, Scotus, Moros, Kouros, Hypnos, Oneiroi, Momus, Moirai, Nemesis, Appetae, Eris*, Amen?

We address these entities as the group, and we declare, Father in Heaven, then we come before You, in the mighty name of Jesus Christ and renounce the Group: the Family of Death, and our associated bloodlines, genetics, ungodly DNA strands, bone marrow, cellular programming, anchors and markers, and all the powers of darkness associated with this, and serve them a bill of divorce.

We pull up the hidden documents detailing every covenant, contract, agreement, certificate, oath, and vow, entangling us and demand that they be stamped with the Blood of Jesus. Amen?

So, in the name of Jesus, we pray that Your Heavenly Hosts will be put on assignment to discover and apprehend every altar or *part* belonging to us that is loyal to The Group, the Family of Death or our associated bloodlines and pray that those parts would be escorted to the feet of the Lion of the Tribe of Judah to be purged of their Group components and completely healed and delivered. Amen?

We now deed all territory in us occupied by The Group, the Family of Death, and our associated genetic code markers, bone marrow, ungodly DNA strands, cellular programming and blood and all sentient intelligences, along with their agendas, connected realms and timelines, over to the Kingdom of God, and invite You, Lord Jesus, to take the throne and to rule over this territory, with Your rod of iron--, we include all essences. Amen?

In the name of Jesus, we now bind all gatekeepers and discover each, and every portal access point associated with The Group, the Family of Death and our associated genetics, markers, bone marrow, ungodly DNA strands, cellular programming, ultra strongholds and blood and all sentient intelligences, along with their agendas, connected realms, timelines, and all associated counterfeit inheritance. Do you agree?

We place the Blood of Jesus and every portal access point, in all timelines, every realm, age and dimension, past, present and future, to infinity, and seal them with the Holy Spirit.

We declare they are put to sleep and permanently deactivated from this point in time and out of time, forward and backward and in every direction, inside out, upside down, back and forth, reversed, inverted and vortexed. We take the Sword of the Spirit, which is the Word of God, and cut ourselves free from The Group: the *Family of Death* and all associated genetic markers, bone marrow, ungodly DNA strands, cellular programming and blood, including all sentient intelligences along with their agendas, related realms, timelines and counterfeit inheritance in Jesus name. Amen?

I return every form of counterfeit inheritance inclusive of promised wealth, position, status, calling, ability, roots, power, genetic code, pride, seed and any other form of counterfeit inheritance, in Jesus' Name.

We sever ourselves from it, and from this point in time, all the time, forward and backward and in every direction, inside out, upside down, back forth, inversed, inverted, vortexed, we speak that we receive our inheritance in Jesus Christ.

We also declare Your Word, which says that the wealth of the wicked is stored up for the just, and speak that the wealth held hostage by The Group: the Family of Death and associated bloodline--we receive it as a recipient of wealth transfer in Jesus' Name.

Furthermore, our physical children are an inheritance in Jesus Christ. We receive them and their redemption, in Jesus Christ.

We renounce all spirit children related to The Group and our associated bloodlines and undo all quantum entanglements involved in their creation. We command their judgment and the purging of the realms they occupy, *by judgment,* through Living Water. Amen?

We now receive a blood transfusion. A new breath of life in Jesus Christ. In the process, we declare that all that is Family of Death's circuitry, nanotech backdoors, front door, side doors, trapdoors, infinite doors, quartz, insects, vampiric structures, reset devices, energy draining devices, implants, wires, cables, chips, computers, chains, programs, backup programs. Power sources, backup power sources, receptors, robots, embryos, fetuses, clones, and eggs are destroyed and all of their residue is purged with Living Water. We also reclaim and receive every part of us that has been imprisoned by The Group or in their realms. Amen?

We appeal to justice and pray that the Family of Death would now reach 100-fold return for all of the evil sown against us, our ancestors and all whom we represent, in the form of justice and judgment and wrath, arrows and lightning hailstones, tsunamis of Living Water and plundering by the Armies of Heaven, in Jesus' Name. Amen?

We now take authority over every evil *spirit* on the inside of us and around us that has been operating due to The Group and our associated bond launch, genetic code markers, ungodly DNA strands, bone marrow, cellular programming assignments, judgments, and blood. We declare you are discovered, apprehended, pierced through, and thrust out of us for judgment.

We also discover every part that is a composite of genetic components of us and others associated with the bloodlines and held together by cords that bind. I declare that the cords are cut, the cords and cords are cut, that all three-fold cords are cut, and then each part is separated into its components. All demonic components and components that are not of us are now bound; we declare that all of them are sent to where the true Lord Jesus Christ sends them. Amen?

Lastly, we pray that every spiritual object, Type 2 device, label, jewel, amulet, necklace, earring, crown, ring, bracelet, charm, garment, center, marker, power source, tracking device, system grid, or branding placed around every part of us in order to anchor in to The Group that is the Family of Death would be consumed in the Holy Fire of Jesus Christ and totally dissolved. We close every door known and unknown, seen and unseen, and call it completely sealed, in Jesus' name. We render this entire confession established everywhere Jehovah is. Amen.

Closing Prayers

Lord, reset, synchronize my destiny clock so that I am on **Your** time, Your calendar for my life, not on Egyptian, bondage or sin time, in the Name of Jesus.

Enemies of God, lose my coordinates, forget my name, lose my location; be drowned in the Red Sea.

Lord, see the Blood of Jesus when you see me, amen.

I resist and have divorced the *Family of Death*; I command it to flee from me, in the Name of Jesus.

I bind the *spirit of death*, and the *Family of Death* in all of its manifestations now, in the Name of Jesus.

I speak to the mountain of sickness, disease, accidents, and incidents, and command it to be cast into the Red Sea with every old Pharoah that pursues after my life, in Jesus' Name.

I plead the Blood of Jesus, over myself, from the top of my head to the soles of my feet. Let the Blood of the Cross stand between me and any dark power delegated against my life.

I curse every work of sickness in my life and dry it out by the root. I plead The Blood against it.

Jesus, who is the Lord and Savior and head of my life –, Jesus, who holds the keys of death, it is in **His** time, only, that I go to Glory.

I evict every dark angel of death from my presence and every evil human agent and every power behind that evil, in the Name of Jesus.

I defeat and paralyze the evil effects of every bacteria, germ, fungus, parasite, cancer, disorder, syndrome, symptom, virus, evil technology or other evil implantation in my body, in the Name of Jesus. You are all condemned go back to the pit from where you came.

I soak my life in the Blood of the Lamb.

I condemn every chattering voice of death which has come to talk me out of the long life that God has promised me. I will not follow your voice, I disobey your voice, I do not heed your evil summons and I do not follow any evil instruction or command that you give me, whether I hear it in the natural, or not. The Blood of Jesus is between you and me, in the Name of Jesus.

I will live and not die; I am not yet satisfied (Psalm 118:17). Get your hands off me. Angels of God, get all evil hands off me, in the Name of Jesus.

Thank You, Lord that you keep my soul among the living and keep my foot from slipping (Psalm 66:9), in Jesus' Name.

I decree every demonic appointment with *Death* is canceled now, in the Name of Jesus. Father, thank You that the power that raised Christ from the dead lives inside me and will quicken my mortal body (Romans 8:11).

Death will have no victory over my life, in the Name of Jesus (1 Corinthians 15:55).

Father, send your Warring Angels to battle every attacking *spirit* and minister strength to me, in the Name of Jesus (Hebrews 1:4).

Thank You, Lord, that You have ransomed my soul from the pit of *Death* and destruction. (Psalm 49:15)

Thank You, Lord that You have destroyed the power of *Death,* in the Name of Jesus (Hebrews 2:14).

Father, thank You, that You have delivered me from the Gates of *Death*, in the Name of Jesus (Psalm 8:13).

Father, thank You for keeping me from falling in the pit of *Death* that the enemy has dug for me (Psalm 30:3).

I walk thru the valley of the shadow of death; I fear no evil, in the Name of Jesus, (Psalm 23).

How great is Your lovingkindness toward me to deliver my soul from death, (Psalm 86:13).

I bind every anti breakthrough, anti-miracle anti-healing *spirit* targeting me, in Jesus' Name.

I command every demon of infirmity to *loose* me, and leave me at once, in Jesus' Name.

I curse diseases, infirmities, and sicknesses, in the Name of Jesus.

I curse the root of sickness at its root, in the Name of Jesus.

I break every word curse, every hex, vex, jinx, spell, incantation, charm, all voodoo, hoodoo, black magic, white magic, red magic, green magic -- every spell, generational curse, every bloodline and family curse, in the Name of Jesus.

I have no fear and I am not dismayed because You are my God and my ever-present Help, and You uphold me by Your Righteous Right Hand, in the Name of Jesus. (Isaiah 41:10)

Thank You Lord, for victory over *death* and the *grave*, in the Name of Jesus. I shall live and not die and declare the glory of the Lord in the land of the living.

I have purpose and destiny; the life of Christ is in me, and I am in Christ. **Father, see The Blood and let all evil pass over me**, protect your investment in me, in the Name of Jesus.

You are the Only Living God and You are the God of the living. I worship and adore You, Lord even in the season of attack, amen.

Thank You for my testimony, in the Name of Jesus.

Lord, thank You for divine angelic detail so that I have no unguarded moment.

Lord, You said when You see The Blood, You will pass over. When You see The Blood, *Death* must pass over, in the Name of Jesus.

I cancel every appointment with *Death*, in the Name of Jesus.

Every satanic undertaker, I bind you and send you back to the pit of hell right now, in the Name of Jesus.

All death contractors, kill each other and then kill yourself, in the Name of Jesus.

Every germ, bacteria, virus, parasite--, everything not of You Lord, die, in the Name of Jesus.

Let every dead organ and cell in my body be resurrected, come back to life, in the Name of Jesus.

Every internal disorder, receive order now, in the Name of Jesus.

Lord, forgive and have Mercy on every negative, destructive word I've spoken over myself causing sickness, disorder, disease, infirmity, or that has invited demons or destruction, and reverse the damage, in the Name of Jesus.

I release myself from every evil covenant for curses I've spoken.

We have power over *Death*, because *Death* is no longer in the hand of the devil but in the hands of Jesus. The Bible says He made an open show of Him and set us free. Thank You, Hallelujah & Amen.

We bind up every spirit of hate, revenge and retaliation and seal up any access point for retaliation of any kind against these prayers, in Jesus' Mighty Name.

We count this work as done, we bless the Lord and seal our decrees and declarations across every timeline, age, realm and dimension, past, present, and future, to infinity, in the Mighty Name of Jesus Christ. Amen.

Acknowledgements

Prayers inspired by mighty prayer warriors of God:

Dr. Anthony & Pastor Nnenna Akerele, for the Pharoah prayer points. https://www.youtube.com/@mountainoffirevirginia

Prayers That Break Curses. and Spells and Release Favor & Breakthrough by Daniel Okpara, https://a.co/d/h9GigVx

Pastor Ikechukwu Chinedum, some points against *Death*. https://www.youtube.com/watch?v=pY3-4P27ab4&t=29s

Kay ElBlessing **Consuming Fire for Fire**: *Disarm Weapons*, https://a.co/d/gSe002X

Dr. Prayer Madueke, **Praying With the Blood of Jesus.**

Portions of the Closing Prayer inspired by Jennifer LeClair, https://www.youtube.com/watch?v=P60Y91Hc5zQ&t=13s

Command the Day: Prayers that Don't Fail, Tella Olayeri. https://a.co/d/9XtXpmO

Dr. Daniel Duvall: *Divorce Death Prayer*, https://www.youtube.com/watch?v=ioW58EhMBUo&t=4146s

Other books by this author:

AK: The Adventures of the Agape Kid

AMONG SOME THIEVES

Ancestral Powers

Blindsided: *Has the Old Man Bewitched You?*

Churchzilla, T*he Wanna-Be, Supposed-to-be Bride of Christ*

Courtroom Warfare @Midnight

Demons Hate Questions

Devil Weapons: Unforgiveness, Bitterness,...

Dream Defilement

Don't Refuse Me, Lord (4 book series)

Every Evil Bird

Evil Touch

Fantasy Spirit Spouse

FAT Demons (The): *Breaking Demonic Curses*

The Fold (4 book series)

    The Fold (Book 1)

    Name Your Seed (Book 2)

    The **Poor Attitudes** of **Money 3**

Do Not Orphan Your Seed

From the Back

got HEALING? Verses for Life

got LOVE? Verses for Life

got HOPE? Verses for Life

got money?

How to Dental Assist

How to Dental Assist 2

Let Me Have A Dollar's Worth

Level the Playing Field

Living for the NOW of God

Lose My Location

Man Safari, *The*

Marriage Ed. *Rules of Engagement & Marriage*

Made Perfect in Love

Motherboard (The)- soul prosperity series 1

Plantation Souls

Power Money: Nine Times the Tithe

The Power of Wealth *(forthcoming)*

Rules of Engagement & Marriage

Seasons of Grief

Seasons of War

Soul Prosperity soul prosperity series 3

Souls Captivity soul prosperity series 2

The Spirit of Poverty

This Is NOT That: How to Keep Demons from Coming At You

Throne of Grace: Courtroom Prayer

Time Is of the Essence

Too Many Wives: *Why You Have Lady Problems*

Tormenting Spirits

Triangular Power *(series)*

    Powers Above

    SUNBLOCK

    Do Not Swear by the Moon

    STARSTRUCK

Upgrade: How to Get Out of Survival Mode (1)

    Toxic Souls (Book 2 of series)

    Legacy (Book 3 of series)

Warfare Prayer Against Beauty Curses

Warfare Prayer Against Poverty

When the Devourer is Rebuked

The Wilderness Romance *(3-book series)*

    The Social Wilderness

    The Sexual Wilderness

    The Spiritual Wilderness

Journals & Devotionals by this author:

The Cool of the Day – for times with God

He Hears Us, Prayer Journal in 4 colors

I Have A Star, Dream Journal kids, teen, adult

I Have A Star, Guided Prayer Journal, Boy, Girl

J'ai une Etoile, Journal des Reves

Let Her Dream, Dream Journal multi colors

Men Shall Dream, Dream Journal, (blue, black)

My Favorite Prayers (multiple covers)

My Sowing Journal (in three colors)

Tengo una Estrella, Diario de Sueños

Illustrated children's books by this author:
Be the Lion (3-book series)
Big Dog (8-book series)
Do Not Say That to Me
Every Apple
Fluff the Clouds
I Love You All Over the World
Imma Dance
The Jump Rope
Kiss the Sun
The Masked Man
Not During a Pandemic
Push the Wind
Slide
Tangled Taffy
What If?
Wiggle, Wiggle; Giggle, Giggle
Worry About Yourself
You Did Not Say Goodbye to Me

www.ingramcontent.com/pod-product-compliance
Lightning Source LLC
Chambersburg PA
CBHW061331040426
42444CB00011B/2867